SUCCESSION PLANNING AND MANAGEMENT

A GUIDE TO ORGANIZATIONAL SYSTEMS AND PRACTICES

SUCCESSION PLANNING AND MANAGEMENT

A GUIDE TO ORGANIZATIONAL SYSTEMS AND PRACTICES

David Berke

Center for Creative Leadership
Greensboro, North Carolina

The Center for Creative Leadership is an international, nonprofit educational institution founded in 1970 to advance the understanding, practice, and development of leadership for the benefit of society worldwide. As a part of this mission, it publishes books and reports that aim to contribute to a general process of inquiry and understanding in which ideas related to leadership are raised, exchanged, and evaluated. The ideas presented in its publications are those of the author or authors.

The Center thanks you for supporting its work through the purchase of this volume. If you have comments, suggestions, or questions about any CCL Press publication, please contact the Director of Publications at the address given below.

Center for Creative Leadership
Post Office Box 26300
Greensboro, North Carolina 27438-6300
336-288-7210 • www.ccl.org

Center for
Creative
Leadership
NORTH AMERICA EUROPE ASIA
www.ccl.org

CCL No. 353

Library of Congress Cataloging-in-Publication Data

Berke, David.
    Succession planning and management : a guide to organizational systems and practices / David Berke.
        p. cm.
    ISBN 1-882197-89-5 (alk. paper)
  1. Executive succession—Planning—Bibliography. 2. Chief executive officers—Selection and appointment—Bibliography. 3. Career development—Bibliography.
4. Executive succession—Planning. 5. Chief executive officers—Selection and appointment. 6. Career development. I. Center for Creative Leadership. II. Title.

    Z7164.O7B32 2005
    [HD38.2]
    016.6584'0711—dc22   2005050107

Table of Contents

Preface

The purpose of succession-related practices is to ensure that there are ready replacements for key positions in an organization. This is so that turnover will not negatively affect organization performance. Interest in succession practices has been increasing over the past few years, spurred by demographic projections, such as those indicating that the number of workers aged 55 and older will increase 47 percent by 2010 (Britt, 2003). Companies must prepare as the baby boomer cohort begins to retire. But there are other trends as well. For example, turnover at the chief executive officer (CEO) level increased 170 percent between 1995 and 2003 (Lucier, Schuyt, & Handa, 2004).

CCL first published an annotated bibliography on succession planning in 1995 (Eastman, 1995). That bibliography focused primarily on the link between succession and management development. This bibliography has a broader scope; it is an update and expansion, commensurate with the maturation of this area of practice. In addition to linkages between succession and development, we also consider representative literature on CEO succession, high potentials, and succession systems and architecture. Each of these four sections is preceded by a brief introduction.

This bibliography is intended to be representative of current and past succession literature related to the four areas mentioned above. It is not intended to be comprehensive or to provide critical commentary. It is hoped that those who use this bibliography will find resources that help them in conceptualizing, planning, and implementing effective succession systems in their organizations.

I want to thank Elisa Hader for her early assistance with this project. I am grateful to Jennifer Deal, Rob Kaiser, Mike Kossler, and Clare Norman for reviewing the manuscript and providing their perspectives. And finally, my thanks to the editors who helped me create a better final version: Joanne Ferguson, Karen Mayworth, Pete Scisco, and Debbie Shoffner.

Introduction

If we consider succession processes along a continuum, replacement planning would be on one end, succession management would be on the other end, and succession planning would be in the middle. As the table below indicates, replacement planning focuses on the identification of replacements for key positions, usually at the top two or three levels of an organization. Basically, it is a forecast. It does not include the deliberate development and preparation of identified successors. If development occurs, it is ad hoc, or perhaps a manager will coach and guide the person he or she believes would be a good replacement. This strategy is based on the assumption that the current manager is also the model for future managers—not necessarily a wise assumption, especially given today's volatile business environment.

At the other end of the continuum is succession management. The key features of this more elaborate, integrated, and systematic approach include the identification and development of high potentials so that when a vacancy occurs in a key position, the organization does not have just a list of potential candidates but a pool of better-prepared candidates. A talent pool or leadership pipeline may be created at most or all management levels. Sometimes organizations will include critical individual contributor positions as well. However, special attention usually is given to those at midsenior levels.

When recruitment, selection, and retention strategies are added, succession management can look very much like talent management (American Productivity & Quality Center [APQC], 2004). When the purpose of succession practices is readiness, talent management and succession management can become indistinguishable.

Continuum of Succession Processes

	Replacement planning	Succession planning	Succession management
Identification of successors	yes	yes	yes
Development of successors	little or none	yes	yes
Managerial levels	top two or three	top two or three	all

Succession management is the most robust approach and the most likely to provide a pool of qualified candidates. It has the added benefit of building capability at several management levels. However, it requires the most resources and an organizational culture that sees the value of talent development and understands how to integrate that into daily operations.

Succession planning has elements of succession management, but its focus tends to be more limited—identifying and developing successors for the top levels of the organization. Additionally, succession planning is often regarded as a less proactive, more static approach than succession management.

The reader should be aware that use of these terms often is inexact: what one company calls succession management, another might call succession planning or talent management.

What Has Changed

In the 1995 bibliography, Eastman lists the elements of an effective succession plan. Those elements are that the plan

- Receives visible support from the CEO and top management
- Is owned by line management and supported by staff
- Is simple and tailored to unique organizational needs
- Is flexible and linked with a strategic business plan
- Evolves from a thorough human resources review process
- Is based upon well-developed competencies and objective assessment of candidates
- Incorporates employee input
- Is part of a broader management development effort
- Includes plans for developmental job assignments
- Is integrated with other human resources systems
- Emphasizes accountability and follow-up

These elements continue to be repeated in much of the current succession literature. Similarly, just as Eastman focused on the link between development and succession, much of the current literature treats development as the core succession process.

What has changed conceptually (and in practice at some companies) is that succession management, in contrast to succession planning, tends to be a more systematic process. One way to think about this distinction is that succession management provides a structure within which development, assessment of progress and fit, and determination of next moves against strategy and bench strength all take place. This assessment and planning process is called the talent review, and it is, in its way, as important as development.

Development is still a core process, but now action learning and cross-functional assignments are accepted as common methodologies. And there is an expectation that various job assignments will be targeted and result in specific learning. Ten years ago, classroom training and workshops were dominant, with much less focus on accountability. Today the emphasis is on blended learning, involving classroom, on-the-job, and e-learning experiences. Additionally, the link between various HR systems and succession has become much more explicit—especially those functions that deal with employment and retention (Corporate Leadership Council, 2003; Kesler, 2002). As mentioned above, one of the main goals of this process is the creation of talent pools or a leadership pipeline for all or most management levels.

Research on high potentials also has progressed since the first bibliography. McCall (1998) talks about the importance of learning as the key distinction between those who are high potentials and those who are not. Lombardo and Eichinger (2000) report on research that also suggests that learning agility is the key. Thus, past performance is only an indication that people will probably perform well at a higher level within the same function. It may *not* be an indication that they will perform well in a different function.

Regardless of the approach, succession processes all act as feeders for position replacements at the top of the organization. In fact, CEO replacement was the original focus of succession planning. It was not until the 1980s that succession planning began to extend to lower management levels (Kesner & Sebora, 1994). Although CEO succession processes often receive media coverage, the processes for selecting a new CEO often are not as visible or available for viewing as processes at lower organizational levels. Thus many of the articles in that section of this bibliography present inferential conclusions.

CEO succession has been a topic of great interest over the past ten years. This is probably due to the celebrity CEOs of the 1990s and the scandals that followed in the wake of the economic recession and collapse of the dot-com market at the turn of the twenty-first century. As mentioned above, between 1995 and 2003, CEO turnover increased 170 percent (Lucier et al., 2004).

Researchers have documented that turnover at the CEO level often has a negative effect on the organization (Wiersema, 2002). They recommend that boards run the CEO selection in ways that are quite similar to selection at lower organizational levels by doing things such as assessing what is needed, choosing the right search committee, and utilizing search firms appropriately (Charan & Useem, 2002; Khurana, 2001).

The articles about CEO succession differ in focus from those in the other sections. Here the concern is on selection, associated political processes, and the implications of all of this on firm performance. In addition to articles discussing current trends (such as Lucier et al., 2004), perennial questions continue to be addressed. Two are whether the CEO should be an insider or an outsider and whether the selection process should be a competition, a visible horse race among insiders.

As for the first question, research suggests that insiders tend to deliver better results than outside successors (Zhang & Rajagopalan, 2004). One study shows that it is a mistake to focus solely on the CEO successor when trying to understand the performance consequences of CEO succession. Post-succession executive turnover tends to have a negative impact on return on assets in outsider successions and a positive impact with certain types of insider successions (Cannella & Shen, 2002).

As for the second question, although a competition may have some appeal, relay succession generally results in better firm performance, primarily because the heir apparent has time to learn the job and build the necessary relationships (Zhang & Rajagopalan, 2004). Relay succession (Vancil, 1987) occurs when the heir apparent is identified well in advance and developed over time—as in a relay race, when one runner hands off the baton to the next. When he or she is appointed CEO, another heir is identified soon after and the process begins again.

Many who work with succession systems deal at the levels below CEO succession. For them as well as those who also work with boards of directors, a succession management system is a complex process, requiring skills and knowledge about building and maintaining organization support and establishing effective processes for developing and assessing people. The books and articles summarized in this bibliography can assist the practitioner in identifying useful references and resources for designing succession processes appropriate for his or her organization.

CEO Succession

CEO succession was the original focus of succession planning (Kesner & Sebora, 1994). It continues to be a topic of great interest, especially given the rise of the celebrity CEO in the 1990s, the economic downturn and corporate scandals that followed, and a significant increase in turnover at the top. Ocasio (1994) points out that one of the effects of shareholder activism is a decrease in the ability of CEOs to institutionalize their power and lengthen their tenure. The author predicts that executive control will be increasingly subject to shifting political coalitions and ongoing political struggles as poor performance highlights the ineffectiveness of a CEO's strategies—one of the primary reasons for selecting a successor from outside the company (also see Miller, 1991).

Lucier et al. (2004) determined that CEO turnover increased 170 percent between 1995 and 2003; in 2004 it dipped below 10 percent world-wide for the first time since 1998. The authors suggest that the cause of this turnover is the focus by boards of directors on performance and their willing-ness to remove those who do not live up to expectations. Wiersema (2002) provides a slightly different perspective on this turnover, suggesting that, more often than not, boards are simply reacting to investor dissatisfaction without fully understanding the issues facing the organization or realizing that the disruptions caused by hurried terminations and by bypassing organization-ally accepted succession processes can cause long-term damage.

Articles and books in this section cover four main areas: the role of the board of directors, the succession process, external versus internal successors, and political processes.

Role of the Board of Directors

The articles relating to the role of the board of directors in the succes-sion process contain a common caution to boards against following fads, bowing to pressure from Wall Street analysts, or selecting a CEO from "central casting" (Charan & Useem, 2002). Instead, the authors remind board members that selection of a new CEO is an opportunity to identify and address critical business needs, not just match boilerplate criteria (Khurana, 2001). Some other key steps include the following (Charan, 2003; Charan & Useem, 2002; Conger & Nadler, 2004; Khurana, 2001; Wiersema, 2002):

- Taking responsibility for the succession process
- Managing the outgoing CEO to ensure that his or her actions do not inadvertently sabotage the success of the new CEO

- Ensuring that the internal talent pipeline is being tended
- Utilizing search firms appropriately
- Selecting the right person for the job that needs to be done, whether that person is an internal or external candidate
- Supporting the new CEO when he or she does what he or she was hired to do

Succession Process

It matters which type of succession process is used. Often CEO succession is an orderly process in which the incumbent steps down to be replaced by an heir apparent who has been identified and groomed for the position. Once the transition to the new CEO has been completed, the process of identifying and grooming the next heir begins again. This is known as relay succession (Vancil, 1987). Conger and Nadler (2004) point to the need for proper development of internal candidates. This means having at least two major enterprise positions, with each assignment lasting three years. These authors also point to the danger that the board will select a second in command whose skill set may be complementary to the CEO's, but not what is needed for the CEO role.

An internal successor will likely have a greater positive impact on firm performance than an outsider when relay succession is used (Zhang & Rajagopalan, 2004). This is the case whether or not the firm is performing well prior to the succession. This is not the case when an organization has decided not to identify an heir apparent, but instead selects from a group of several internal candidates. The larger the pool of internal candidates, the less likely it is that an heir apparent will be named. In that situation, when a firm has not performed well, an outsider is more likely to have a positive impact on firm performance than someone chosen from a group of several internal candidates.

External versus Internal Successors

Generally speaking, outside successors are recommended when a significant change is needed. The belief is that an outsider can bring a fresh perspective unencumbered by old political alliances and strategic and operational approaches that are out of touch with the current market (Andrews, 2001; Guthrie & Datta, 1998; Miller, 1991).

From another perspective, these constraints (organizational knowledge and a strong network) are the tools an insider would use to move change through an organizational system. An outsider will need at least six months to two years to develop this knowledge and network, and until then he or she will be vulnerable to possible board impatience or dissatisfaction and/or to opposition from incumbent senior management (Cannella & Shen, 2001).

While it is possible to think of examples in which an outsider brought necessary change—Lou Gerstner at IBM is among the most prominent—the benefit of choosing an outsider is far from certain, especially when considering financial results. Several authors say that external successors do not necessarily deliver better results than those they replace (Cannella & Shen, 2002; Lucier et al., 2004; Wiersema, 2002; Zhang & Rajagopalan, 2004). Additionally, when an outsider becomes CEO following planned turnover—usually retirement—the impact on firm performance is quite often negative (Andrews, 2001).

Another factor to consider is industry fit. Some industries can more easily accommodate outsiders than others (Datta, Guthrie, & Rajagopalan, 2002). These authors found that firms in highly concentrated capital-intensive industries are more likely to have CEOs with high levels of industry-specific experience. The opposite is the case for firms in high-growth and differentiated industries.

Political Processes

Some observers assume that an inside successor will continue the practices of his or her predecessor. Cannella and Shen (2002) point out that this may not be the case and that it is a mistake to focus solely on the CEO successor when trying to understand the performance consequences of CEO succession. Post-succession executive turnover matters. It tends to have a negative impact on return on assets with outsider successions and a positive impact with internal successions when the internal successor is a person who has decided to challenge the practices of the departing CEO.

Similarly, being named heir apparent does not necessarily mean becoming CEO. Cannella and Shen (2001) point out that when the CEO is powerful and the firm is prospering, heirs apparent are more likely to leave because the CEO acts to retain power. However, when the CEO is powerful and the firm is not doing so well, heirs apparent are more likely to remain. These authors also point out that outside board members have an important role. When the firm is doing well, outside directors are more likely to encourage heirs apparent to remain with the firm and to push for promotion against a strong CEO. When a firm is not doing well, directors may view heirs critically; if their performance is not strong, they are not likely to be promoted to CEO. The reason for not promoting them is that it is easier and less expensive to remove an underperforming heir than to remove an underperforming CEO.

Annotated Bibliography

Andrews, K. Z. (2001). The performance impact of new CEOs: When a CEO departs, choosing the best successor depends on why the incumbent left. *MIT Sloan Management Review, 42*(2), 14.

The author summarizes a study conducted by Rakesh Khurana and Nitin Nohria on the performance consequences of CEO turnover. This research links two elements of CEO turnover: the circumstances of a CEO's departure and whether the successor comes from inside or outside the company.

The researchers divided turnover into four categories:

- Voluntary, or natural, turnover followed by internal succession
- Forced turnover followed by inside succession
- Voluntary turnover followed by an outsider
- Forced turnover followed by an outsider

The researchers found that voluntary turnover followed by insider succession did not tend to result in a change in company performance. Replacing the CEO with an insider led to a continuation of the status quo. The same was true when an insider replaced a CEO who was dismissed; the insider was too much a part of the political and operational status quo, even though the dismissal was a strong indication that change was needed.

In contrast, when an outsider replaced a fired CEO, the researchers found that company performance rose by more than 4 percent during the following three years. Citing Lou Gerstner at IBM as an example, the researchers make the point that outsiders lack the baggage that constrains inside successors from making necessary changes. However, when an outsider replaces a retiring CEO, the result is different. In that case, performance dropped 6 percent. The researchers suggest that the reasons are that the CEO's natural departure does not give the outsider a platform from which to take action. Additionally, in this situation, outsiders often face opposition from incumbent senior management.

Finally, the authors point out that the board of directors has a responsibility to determine whether the senior team will support the new CEO and the changes he or she may want to make, and if not, whether the new CEO will have necessary power and authority to select people who will.

✳ ✳ ✳

Cannella, A. A., Jr., & Shen, W. (2001). So close and yet so far: Promotion versus exit for CEO heirs apparent. *Academy of Management Journal, 44,* 252–270.

The authors view succession as the result of a political process reflecting the distribution of power among the three parties most directly involved: the incumbent CEO, outside members of the board of directors, and the heir apparent.

When the CEO is powerful and the firm is doing well, heirs apparent are less likely to make it to the top because the powerful CEO will take steps to avoid loss of power, prestige, etc. Thus, the heirs apparent are more likely to leave before a transfer of power can occur. When the CEO is powerful and the firm is not performing well, heirs apparent are more likely to remain with the firm.

Outside directors often monitor the process and counterbalance the CEO. Outside director power was not related to heir apparent promotion. But it did impact heir apparent departures. When powerful outside directors are in place, heirs are more likely to remain when the firm is doing well; outside directors are more likely to support their staying with the firm and may push for promotion against the strong CEO. When the firm is not doing well, directors may view heirs apparent very critically; when current performance is questionable, promotion to CEO becomes increasingly doubtful. Even when the CEO is weak or not performing well, it is easier and less costly to remove a weak heir apparent than the CEO.

✳ ✳ ✳

Cannella, A. A., Jr., & Shen, W. (2002). Revisiting the performance consequences of CEO succession: The impacts of successor type, postsuccession senior executive turnover, and departing CEO tenure. *Academy of Management Journal, 45,* 717–734.

A common belief is that insiders will continue the policies of the CEOs they replace while outsiders will be brought in to change the organization and improve its performance.

The authors suggest that while outsiders usually are brought in to improve a company's performance, it is not entirely correct to say that all insiders who assume the CEO position intend to continue the policies of their predecessors. Cannella and Shen say that some, called followers, will do that while others, called contenders, will act much like outsiders and try to change the company and improve its performance. A contender gets the CEO position by convincing the board that the incumbent CEO is not up to the demands of the job.

This study looks at the impact on company performance when outsiders and contenders become CEOs. The study also looks at the impact of post-succession executive turnover on company performance and links this turnover with the type of CEO successor.

Neither outsiders nor contenders tend to have a positive impact on firm performance. The authors suggest that this is the case for contenders because, even though their aim is strategic change, they remain constrained by their internal social networks within the firm. Unless they can restructure their executives groups, they are not likely to be successful. The opposite is the case for outsiders. It is the high level of post-succession turnover at the senior executive level that leads to a negative impact on firm performance.

Thus, the authors suggest, it is a mistake to focus solely on the CEO successor when trying to understand the performance consequences of CEO succession. Post-succession executive turnover matters. It has a negative impact on firm return on assets in outsider successions and a positive impact with contender successions.

✳ ✳ ✳

Charan, R. (2003, Winter). Boardroom supports. *Strategy + Business,* pp. 32–36.

The author highlights three key points for boards to consider when selecting a new CEO:

- Boards need to select the right person for the job that needs to be done at the time; specific criteria should be developed and used for the selection.

- Boards should ensure that the internal leadership pipeline is being well tended. However, when the time comes to select a CEO, boards should choose the person whom they believe will do the job best regardless of whether that person is an internal or external candidate.

- When a board has hired a CEO to implement a particular strategy, the board should stand by the CEO when he or she does what he or she was hired to do.

✳ ✳ ✳

Charan, R., & Useem, J. (2002, November 18). The five pitfalls of CEO succession. *Fortune, 146,* 78.

The authors, citing an unnamed survey, say that 45 percent of boards of directors have no process for grooming potential CEOs. That sets them up for five pitfalls:

- Letting the CEO play kingmaker: The authors suggest that boards should take charge of the succession process. A minimum of six years before the CEO's anticipated retirement, the board should demand a list of candidates and follow this with regular briefings on how those candidates' skills are being tested. Outside directors should meet with top contenders as they emerge. The authors also recommend a periodic census of the leadership pools at all levels to spot future stars.

- Using boilerplate criteria: The authors say that the board's task is to find someone with the right skills for the job, not someone who meets central casting's idea of a leader. Boards need to be clear about business challenges and the skills needed to meet those challenges.

- Letting headhunters run the selection process: By assembling a slate of qualified candidates, executive recruiters can play a valuable role. However, the board needs to stay in charge of the selection process. They should not allow headhunters to rush the selection. When finalists have been chosen, directors should set aside sufficient time—the authors suggest two days—to interview the candidates thoroughly. The interviews should not be wooing sessions.

- Succumbing to fads: Hiring outsiders is the current fashion. Some-times it makes sense to do this, but often this is not the best ap-proach. Outsiders are more expensive than insiders and, on average, perform no better. The board has considerably less information about outside candidates than internal candidates. A fixation on outside saviors undervalues in-house talent and may be a symptom of the board's anxiety to please Wall Street. Citing Michael Armstrong at ATT and George Fisher at Kodak as examples, the authors point out that the surges in stock price that accompanied their appointments were short lived.

- Keeping Elvis in the building: After the board picks a new CEO, the old one must leave. Continuing presence in the building or on the board can undermine the successor's efforts.

* * *

Conger, J. A., & Nadler, D. A. (2004). When CEOs step up to fail. *MIT Sloan Management Review, 45*(3), 50–56.

This article summarizes research aimed at clarifying reasons that new CEOs fail early in their tenures. The authors identify three broad reasons:

- Actions of the outgoing CEO
- A flawed succession process
- CEO's orientation—a focus on content or on context

With regard to the first, the authors give three key reasons: the outgoing CEO may not want to leave the job, may not be willing to address new problems, or may push for a public accomplishment that serves his or her own needs more than the needs of the organization.

With regard to the second, the authors point to the need for proper development of internal candidates. For the authors this means a minimum of two major enterprise positions, with each assignment lasting about three years. The authors also point to the dangers of the board's selecting a second in command whose skill set, while complementary to the CEO's, may not be what is needed in the CEO role. The authors suggest that work on succession needs to begin—or continue—at the start of a CEO's tenure. The CEO needs to track the progress of those in the succession pool and look for emerging talent.

With regard to the third item above, the authors distinguish between those CEOs who focus on content and those who focus on context. By content the authors mean the business itself, its core technology, financial structure, business portfolio, etc. These CEOs may rely on specific functional strengths. By context, the authors mean the environment and processes needed to produce the best decisions. The authors suggest that content-oriented CEOs are a better choice in time of crisis or when there has been a major shift or change in an industry's business model. Otherwise a context-oriented CEO is a better choice. They suggest that context skills be part of the criteria for CEO selection.

The authors also have some suggestions for the board on how to collaborate with their CEO on the succession process.

- They need to monitor whether the CEO is approaching succession from an emotional perspective and find ways to mitigate that.

- They should work with the CEO to identify the candidates who are best qualified to handle the strategic challenges facing the business rather than favor those candidates who are most like the CEO.
- They should ensure that there is a succession plan and associated processes in place and operating at all times, and they should focus on development of internal candidates.
- They should insist on a transition process with appropriate length and structure—in which the heir apparent has the opportunity to create a context or demonstrate an inability to do that.
- Finally, the board should continue to monitor the new CEO's ability to build context.

✳ ✳ ✳

Datta, D. K., Guthrie, J. P., & Rajagopalan, N. (2002). Different industries, different CEOs? A study of CEO career specialization. *Human Resource Planning, 25*(2), 14–25.

This article summarizes the results of research focused on determining whether there is a relationship between CEO career specialization by industry, firm, or functional area and particular industry characteristics. The authors found that CEOs' backgrounds vary predictably as a function of industry characteristics. Thus firms in highly concentrated, usually capital-intensive, industries are more likely to have CEOs with high levels of function-, firm-, or industry-specific experiences. The opposite is the case for firms in high-growth and differentiated industries.

✳ ✳ ✳

Guthrie, J. P., & Datta, D. K. (1998). Corporate strategy, executive selection, and firm performance. *Human Resource Management, 37,* 101–115.

This article summarizes research exploring the value of a CEO's experience with the firm he or she leads. The strategic staffing literature emphasizes the importance of matching executive characteristics with a company's strategy. Other research and theory suggest that as a business expands into multiple units, the CEO's job changes from deep knowledge of the core business to portfolio management.

This research was aimed at determining whether

- Firms pursuing different corporate diversification strategies select CEOs whose experience fits the strategy

- Organizational tenure levels (the CEO's tenure with the company) of selected CEOs are related to subsequent organizational performance
- The relationship between CEO tenure levels and subsequent firm performance is moderated by the extent of diversification

Results showed that those who had shorter tenure with a company or who were considered outsiders tended to have better results than those who had longer tenure with the company or who were considered insiders. The authors suggest that environmental turbulence increases the need for regular reexamination of the status quo and for innovation and change. Firm-specific information may impede the need to adapt.

✷ ✷ ✷

Kesner, I. F., & Sebora, T. C. (1994). Executive succession: Past, present, and future. *Journal of Management, 20*, 327–372.

The authors review the history of research related to succession. This is done in three phases:

- Initial work in the 1960s, with reference to some work in the 1950s
- Theory building and empirical investigation in the 1970s
- Great expansion of the field in the 1980s

The authors divide the work of the first phase into four general categories:

- Successor origin: Internal or external?
- Organization size and succession rates: The larger the company, the more frequent the succession rates.
- Succession rate and post-succession performance: Three different theories were proposed—performance improved following succession; frequent succession was disruptive and therefore led to poor performance; and, in response to this second theory, causality could not be demonstrated. The authors of this third theory proposed "ritual scapegoating" as an explanation. These hypotheses served as the basis for research in the following decade and encouraged researchers to investigate whether leadership matters.
- Succession contingencies: Researchers investigated individual characteristics of the successor, such as leadership style and organizational characteristics.

During the second phase, researchers continued examination of the areas above, often further clarifying and expanding on work previously done. For example, some researchers recognized that outside succession could come from inside the company when the successor was someone who was not a member of the predecessor's coalition or in-group. Political dynamics of the succession process began to be examined.

Additionally, researchers began to examine the role of corporate boards and their decision-making processes. Successor origin work expanded to include type of industry and industry experience of successors, leading to work on fit and strategic staffing.

During the third phase, research expanded significantly in the areas mentioned above. In addition, researchers began to examine succession-planning systems and to expand their investigations below the CEO level. Despite increased activity and more precise research methodologies, the authors were unable to identify a consistent model of antecedents, consequences, or contingencies.

The authors conclude their extensive literature review by suggesting areas for future research.

✳ ✳ ✳

Khurana, R. (2001). Finding the right CEO: Why boards often make poor choices. *MIT Sloan Management Review, 43*(1), 91–95.

The author identifies seven pitfalls common in CEO searches and ways to avoid these pitfalls. They are as follows:

- Missing the chance for organizational introspection. The board should avoid a rush to judgment. CEO selection provides the board with an opportunity to reassess company goals and objectives, diagnose the source(s) of key problems, and determine the skills and experience candidates need to reach specific organizational goals. A specific strategic purpose may help a committee choose a candidate based on position requirements instead of personality.

- Choosing the wrong search committee. Board members often have significant demands on their time and attention. Too often that means that those who have the time for search committee membership receive the assignment. The author suggests that search committees consist of directors who are deeply familiar with the company, its problems, and its future challenges. Additionally, committee members should represent a variety of disciplines and/or backgrounds to help minimize the "hire someone like me" syndrome.

- Outsourcing critical steps. It is common to hire a search firm. This is often done on the assumption that the search firm will do everything up to the point where the actual hiring takes place. The author points out that search firms have some important limitations: they will know general requirements but usually will not know the company or its challenges and problems intimately, and they will have factual information about the candidate but probably not important details about the candidates they are proposing. The author suggests that most board members probably are more capable than a search firm in evaluating CEO talent and most can use their networks to identify candidates and get to know them. The author suggests that search firms are best used for adding one or two candidates to those identified by board members; managing expectations of candidates and companies; gauging candidate interest without naming the company; and sometimes helping negotiate salary, stock options, and severance contracts.

- Defining the candidate pool too narrowly. Many times the candidate pool is limited by the search committee's belief that a new CEO must have prior experience as a CEO or by concern with what the media or market analysts might say. This can unnecessarily limit identification of talented candidates and significantly reduce options.

- Equating candidates with their past companies. It is a mistake to think that a candidate from a successful company will be successful as the CEO in a new company. The candidates' influence on his or her current company's performance may be difficult to determine. Factors contributing to a candidate's past success are not all visible, nor are flaws.

- Overestimating the value of insider or outsider status. There are pros and cons to selecting an insider or an outsider. Neither insider nor outsider status is a guarantee of success.

- Accepting false assumptions. Many search committee members have unexamined assumptions that may hamper effective decision making. Even if decisions are made on more realistic criteria, political compromise and the process of elimination may leave a company with a mediocre final choice.

✳ ✳ ✳

Lucier, C., Schuyt, R., & Handa, J. (2004, Summer). CEO succession 2003:
  The perils of good governance. *Strategy + Business,* pp. 70–86.

  The article reports on the results of Booz Allen Hamilton's annual study
of global CEO succession. For the first time since 1998, CEO turnover
worldwide was under 10 percent. The authors temper this by noting that CEO
dismissals increased 170 percent from 1995 to 2003. They attribute this to a
focus on performance and a willingness to dismiss those CEOs who do not
perform to expectations. The authors note that this focus appears to be contributing to lower average shareholder returns since companies are having
difficulty finding qualified internal replacements—they say that external
replacements deliver poorer returns than insiders. Additionally, the authors
contend that the current corporate governance focus on separating the CEO
and chairman roles also leads to lower returns. The report also looks at trends
by global region.

  Key findings include the following:

- In 2003, 9.5 percent of the world's 2,500 largest companies changed
  CEOs. Some of this turnover was planned, a bit more was due to the
  results of mergers and acquisitions, and the rest was due to firing for
  poor performance. This is the first time since 1998 that CEO turnover was under 10 percent. The primary reason was a decline in
  CEOs being fired for poor performance.
- Involuntary CEO succession in North America (U.S. and Canada)
  was 31 percent in 2003, down from 39 percent in 2002.
- Almost half of CEO turnover in Europe was performance related.
- Splitting the CEO and chairman roles does not lead to higher shareholder returns. This is contrary to the position being promoted by
  those leading reform of corporate governance.
- Over the six years of this study, 28 percent of departing CEOs were
  also chairman; 55 percent held only the CEO title.
- Outside successors tend not to be successful: in North America in
  2003, 55 percent of outsiders left involuntarily; in Europe it was 70
  percent.
- Internal successors tend to be the best-performing CEOs.
- Average tenure for CEOs who left their positions in 2003 was 7.6
  years—among the lowest since 1995.
- The younger a person is when named CEO, the more likely it is
  that he or she will be fired. The average starting age for the group

experiencing forced turnover was 49. CEOs who retired voluntarily were five years older on average when they were hired as CEOs.

＊ ＊ ＊

Miller, D. (1991). Stale in the saddle: CEO tenure and the match between organization and environment. *Management Science, 37*(1), 34–52.

Miller reports on research showing that long-tenured CEOs in nondiversified firms tend to lead organizations whose strategies are misaligned with their environment, resulting in poor organization performance. Miller connects length of position tenure to an increasing misalignment, suggesting that gestalts will change greatly only when a new CEO unencumbered by the old gestalt is brought in from outside the firm.

＊ ＊ ＊

Ocasio, W. (1994). Political dynamics and the circulation of power: CEO succession in U.S. industrial corporations, 1960–1990. *Administrative Science Quarterly, 39*, 285–312.

The author views the firm as a political coalition with executives as the primary political brokers. This article examines the political dynamics of executive control over the organization's dominant coalition as reflected in the CEO's ability to retain power. The author conducted research comparing two models of political power: circulation of power and institutionalization of power.

The circulation of power model emphasizes the impermanence of executive control through shifting political coalitions and ongoing political struggles. These would emerge during periods of poor economic performance, which would tend to highlight the obsolescence of strategies adopted by the CEO. Thus CEO tenure is also a factor.

The institutionalization of power model describes processes that may lead to the institutionalization and perpetuation of power. In this model, the CEO's power is likely to increase the period of incumbency as CEO and board member. In this model, the CEO's power is most evident during times of economic adversity, as more powerful CEOs will consolidate their power to maintain authority and position.

The study showed that the political dynamics of CEO succession between 1960 and 1990 reflected both models, with increasing rates of CEO succession up to the beginning of a CEO's second decade in position. CEOs may experience both increasing legitimacy and obsolescence during their tenure, but results indicate that for average CEOs, it takes more than a decade for the legitimacy of their power to decrease and the potential of rival political coalitions to emerge. Thus the circulation model appears within the first decade and the institutionalization model after that.

Results also showed that the institutionalization model was more prevalent before the mid-1980s, when leveraged buyouts and other forms of shareholder activism became more prevalent. The author predicts that the circulation of power model will become more dominant.

Additionally, when adverse economic conditions combine with long board tenure by the CEO, the CEO tends to be more vulnerable to challenges —not less, as might be assumed.

✳ ✳ ✳

Shen, W., & Cannella, A., Jr. (2002). Power dynamics within top management and their impacts on CEO dismissal followed by inside succession. *Academy of Management Journal, 45,* 1195–1205.

According to the authors, CEO succession usually involves an orderly process in which the incumbent steps down at an agreed-upon time and is replaced by an heir apparent who has been identified in advance and groomed for the position. When a CEO is dismissed, usually within the context of poor performance, outside directors often initiate the action and appoint an outsider as successor.

This article focuses on a subset of successions in which conflicts within top management lead to the CEO being dismissed and an insider being appointed as successor. The authors provide a general overview of how interest conflicts and competition develop between a CEO and other senior executives and then identify four factors that they believe particularly reflect the power dynamics that arise between the CEO and senior executives.

Poor company performance often leads top management to band together to defend itself. Sometimes, however, poor firm performance can be fertile ground for power struggles to develop between senior executives and the CEO. The authors name three contributing factors: ambition and desire to "run one's own shop"; the power, prestige, and benefits that accrue to a CEO; and the negative impact that poor firm performance has on the senior executives' reputations and value in the external job market.

With this as a context, the authors identify four factors that increase the likelihood of a CEO from outside the company being dismissed and an internal person succeeding the dismissed CEO. The four factors are as follows:

- CEO origin—Inside successors are more likely to have a strong internal network and support from both the board and non-CEO executives. Outside successors usually lack the network and, because they often are brought in to initiate change, there is a built-in conflict with the senior executives because change often means restructuring top management groups.

- CEO tenure—It takes time for any new CEO to become established and even more time when the new CEO is an outsider. Until new CEOs can demonstrate competence and meet the expectations of the board and their subordinate executives, they will be much weaker than established CEOs and vulnerable to power contests with rival executives. An insider is more likely to have some level of support from executive management as well as the board.

- Non-CEO inside directors—Inside directors are in a position to develop relationships with the board that may facilitate a viable challenge to the CEO, reduce reliance of outside directors on the CEO for information about the firm, and narrow the power gap between the executives and the CEO.

- Senior executive (non-CEO) stock ownership—Stock ownership among senior executives serves to align managerial actions with shareholder interests, thus reducing what are called agency problems. Within the context of this article, senior executive stock ownership typically does not provide enough voting power to oust a CEO. But it does increase the credibility of senior executives' concerns about CEO performance, their influence in selection of an inside successor following dismissal, and their financial incentives to monitor the CEO and thus weaken his or her influence over them.

✳ ✳ ✳

Vancil, R. F. (1987). *Passing the baton: Managing the process of CEO succession*. Boston: Harvard Business School Press.

Based on interviews with forty-eight executives, the author describes the typical process of succession as well as the CEO's succession-related responsibilities, such as developing a pool of candidates and designing the process for selecting his or her successor. These matters fall within the broader context of having overall responsibility for organization continuity and change. The latter is more likely to occur with an outside succession; the former with an internal candidate.

The author says the most common pattern of succession is analogous to a relay race, during which the CEO and his or her successor work in tandem until the CEO passes the baton (the role of CEO) to the successor and then the process begins again with his or her successor. More specifically, there are four stages in a CEO's career: president, president and CEO, CEO and chairman, and chairman. During the first two stages, the president (and future CEO) is paired with his or her predecessor; during the last two stages, the now current CEO is paired with his or her successor.

The author reports that this approach has the virtue of providing the heir apparent with the opportunity to build his or her own team and to develop a corporate perspective that includes outside stakeholders. (In some ways, this is also a probation period for the heir apparent.) This period also provides other senior managers with time to assess their expectations.

A competition, or horse race, is a less common succession process but one that is more often reported in the business press. Typically, a competition results in one winner and several losers.

✳ ✳ ✳

Wiersema, M. (2002). Holes at the top: Why CEO firings backfire. *Harvard Business Review, 80*(12), 70–77.

The author reports on research regarding the effects of the dismissals of increasing numbers of CEOs in recent years. In essence, she says that most companies perform no better in terms of standard financial measures after a dismissal than in the years leading up to the dismissal. Additionally, the disruption caused by hurried firings and by bypassing organizationally accepted succession processes can cause damage that may last for years.

The author places responsibility for this situation with the board of directors. Reacting to investor dissatisfaction, the board dismisses a CEO without thinking through what must happen next. They are left with the full responsibility of filling the position when they have neither the time nor a sufficiently deep strategic understanding of the business to give due diligence to choosing a replacement. This lack of understanding also means that they cannot adequately advise a search firm on the requirements. Concern over restoring investor confidence, rather than doing what is right for the business, often leads to poor selections. And because the board members often do not understand the issues that drive performance, they also do not understand the problems that need to be solved. The result is that the issues that created problems under the old CEO often continue under the new one.

The author says that there are some things a board can do that will lead to a positive outcome for the company. The board should develop a better understanding of the business and the context within which the business operates, be more concerned about a replacement's fit with the strategies and goals of the business, and take an active role in overseeing the new CEO and the performance of the company.

✳ ✳ ✳

Zhang, Y., & Rajagopalan, N. (2004). When the known devil is better than an unknown god: An empirical study of the antecedents and consequences of relay CEO successions. *Academy of Management Journal, 47,* 483–500.

The authors report on research aimed at investigating three types of CEO successions: relay successions, inside nonrelay successions, and outside successions. (See the summary of Vancil, 1987, for a description of relay succession.)

The findings:

- The authors found that firms are less likely to designate and groom an heir apparent if there are multiple inside candidates for the CEO position. They are more likely to continue to assess all internal candidates and select one without first designating that person as heir apparent.

- When a firm is performing well, it is more likely to designate an heir apparent and groom that person. When a firm is not performing well, that is less likely.

- Relay successions contributed to better post-succession firm performance than nonrelay inside succession and outside succession. This also applied when the company was facing challenging conditions (i.e., the firm was not performing well or the industry was changing in some fundamental ways). A nonrelay inside succession had no more impact on the firm's performance than an outside succession. The authors speculate that the value of the relay succession is the opportunity for the heir apparent to learn important lessons and develop additional competencies before assuming the CEO position. This is especially true when the firm is facing difficult challenges.

- The authors point out that one of the implications of their findings is that outside succession may not result in better firm performance. This is because outsiders are likely to lack the firm-specific knowledge needed to formulate and implement strategic change. Additionally, outside successors may find it difficult to get support from senior executives within the firm. The exception is the case of high levels of instability within a firm's industry segment where outside successors have a greater positive impact than nonrelay inside successors.

Development

Development is one of the core processes used in succession management systems. Articles and books in this section deal with the process needed for effective development and the focus or content of that development. Each of the referenced books or articles in this section contains great detail and often case studies to assist the reader.

There appears to be general agreement that the process for development should include the following:

- Linking development to the organization strategy (APQC, 1999; Corporate Leadership Council, 2001; Lombardo & Eichinger, 2002; McCall, 1998)
- Developing a competency model, often by adapting preexisting competency models (Corporate Leadership Council, 2001; Lombardo & Eichinger, 2002)
- Specifying competencies in terms of outcomes for needs assessment, design of development initiatives, and evaluation of development initiatives (Lewis, 2003)
- Ensuring that executive and line management are accountable for development (APQC, 1999; Corporate Leadership Council, 2001; Lombardo & Eichinger, 2002)
- Ensuring that development has a large component of learning through experience (APQC, 1999; Corporate Leadership Council, 2001; Lombardo & Eichinger, 2002; McCall, 1998)
- Linkage of the development effort to the organization's succession and high potential processes (APQC, 1999; Corporate Leadership Council, 2001; Lombardo & Eichinger, 2002; McCall, 1998)

Barrett and Beeson (2002) provide the results of a Conference Board study to identify the critical roles business leaders will play and the key skills they will need by 2010. Another book (Giber, Carter, & Goldsmith, 2000) provides case studies describing fifteen management development programs from determination of need to evaluation. Finally, the Corporate Leadership Council (2003) approaches the development question by distinguishing between those companies the CLC has determined are top-tier leadership organizations and those that are not. Recommendations in this book complement those above and also reflect more of a talent management perspective.

Annotated Bibliography

American Productivity & Quality Center. (1999). *Leadership development: Building executive talent*. Houston, TX: Author.

This report contains the results of a benchmarking study aimed at identifying strong or innovative leadership development processes. Thirteen key findings emerged within four general categories:

- Creating a leadership development process: The key findings in this area relate to aligning development with business strategy, emphasizing both business experience and human resources, and balancing an internal focus with ongoing awareness of external forces.

- Identifying the leadership pool: The key findings in this area relate to defining leadership competencies and developing talent from within instead of bringing it in from the outside.

- Engaging future leaders: The key findings in this area relate to linking development to the succession-planning process, not substituting technology for face-to-face interaction, and emphasizing that the goal of leadership development is action, not just knowledge.

- Understanding the effect of leadership development: The key findings in this area relate to recognizing that leadership development is costly and necessary and that it is essential to assess the impact of development efforts.

✳ ✳ ✳

Barrett, A., & Beeson, J. (2002). *Developing business leaders for 2010*. New
York: The Conference Board.

The authors summarize research aimed at defining challenges anticipated for business leaders in 2010. Only a third of respondents to the survey
rated their leadership capacity to respond to sudden changes or meet business
challenges as excellent or good.

Critical roles for 2010:

- Master strategist
- Change manager
- Relationship builder or network manager
- Talent developer

Key skills for 2010:

- Cognitive ability
- Analytical ability
- Strategic thinking
- Decision making in an ambiguous environment
- Influence and persuasion
- Management in a diverse environment—cultural and generational
  differences

The report also covers anticipated derailers and various types of leadership development strategies and includes detailed case studies on some of
those strategies. There also is discussion that highlights that leadership development is not a risk-free activity. Suggestions are made to manage those risks.

✲ ✲ ✲

Corporate Leadership Council. (2001). *The leadership imperative: Strategies
for increasing leadership bench strength*. Washington, DC: Author.

The primary focus of this report is on case studies illustrating the CLC's
recommended strategies for increasing bench strength. Overall, the report
suggests five strategies within two categories.

The first category is focusing development resources on critical leadership capabilities. Within this category are two strategies:

- Defining skills and attributes most needed for effective leadership
- Proactive management of leadership development to meet future
  needs

There are two detailed case studies for each strategy.

The second category is enabling efficient delivery of highest-impact development activities. Within this category are three strategies:

- Providing managers with the tools to accelerate development of leaders and holding the managers accountable for development

- Using technology and other means to support ongoing leadership development outside the classroom

- Creating development plans that address key individual areas and the organization's most significant capability needs

There are two detailed case studies for the first two strategies and one detailed case study for the last.

✳ ✳ ✳

Corporate Leadership Council. (2003). *Hallmarks of leadership success: Strategies for improving leadership quality and executive readiness.* Washington, DC: Author.

This report contains the results and recommendations of a research project for which 276 organizations worldwide provided data. The same data set was used for the CLC's *High-Impact Succession Management* report, discussed below. This report identifies what distinguishes top-tier leadership organizations and what organizations can do to increase their chances of becoming top-tier leadership organizations.

The report identifies seven hallmarks of top-tier leadership organizations and thirty-four critical drivers allocated among the seven hallmarks. The seven hallmarks are as follows:

- Senior executive commitment to development

- Organizational reinforcement of development

- Hiring for organizational compatibility

- Exacting performance standards

- Full business exposure for rising executives

- Selecting successors for leadership ability

- Focusing on scarce skills and fit with position

The report lists the drivers in rank order by impact. And for each hallmark, the report shows which critical drivers are used most and which are not—and might therefore warrant increased focus. For example, the two critical drivers for the last hallmark, focusing on scarce skills and fit with position, are to include people or positions hard to find in the external labor market and to identify successors for specific positions versus using pools. Data from the study show that 12.8 percent of organizations do the first and 33.5 percent of organizations do the second. The authors recommend an increase in both.

✳ ✳ ✳

Giber, D., Carter, L., & Goldsmith, M. (Eds.). (2000). *Linkage Inc.'s best practices in leadership development handbook.* San Francisco: Jossey-Bass.

This book contains descriptions of leadership development programs from fifteen organizations, both for profit and not for profit or governmental. Using a case study approach, the book provides various tools and models that can be used as references when designing a development program. The cases follow the entire cycle of development from needs assessment and building a business case to evaluating the effectiveness of the initiative.

✳ ✳ ✳

Lewis, B. O. (2003, January). Organizational assessments: Aligning learning with strategic directions. *Chief Learning Officer.* Retrieved May 16, 2005, from http://www.clomedia.com/content/templates/clo_feature_ls.asp ?articleid=93&zoneid=64

The author proposes the use of competencies at the level of training objectives as the basis for assessing individual development needs against current business conditions and/or projected future business directions. She suggests relating competencies to business outcomes to demonstrate the return on investment of developing the new skills described by the competencies. She also suggests using competency profiles to identify individuals with the abilities and other desirable attributes needed for higher-level management and engaging their managers in developing them for the company succession effort.

She says that aggregate competency profiles can provide a baseline description of current capability and, when compared against company strategy, can indicate important gaps that need to be addressed. She proposes that when a company enables its employees to take responsibility for planning much of their own development, the company is also enabling culture change.

✳ ✳ ✳

Lombardo, M. M., & Eichinger, R. W. (2002). *The leadership machine: Architecture to develop leaders for any future.* Minneapolis, MN: Lominger, Inc.

The authors contend that there are four fundamentals regarding management and leadership development and that these have not changed and do not change.

- The competencies or skills that matter for leading in new and different situations
- How these skills are learned and developed
- Who is equipped to learn these skills
- What it takes to make skill development work

The authors describe their recommendations for each of the above and provide steps for implementation.

✳ ✳ ✳

McCall, M. W., Jr. (1998). *High flyers: Developing the next generation of leaders.* Boston: Harvard Business School Press.

This book describes an approach to executive development driven by an organization's strategic business needs and based on the idea that most learning occurs from experience on the job. The author's perspective is that leaders can be developed and that even those born with "the right stuff" benefit from development and an environment that supports development. The author suggests that the ability to learn may be the most important attribute of potential leaders and discusses organization mechanisms, such as succession planning, for matching people and development experiences. The author also discusses the elements that make for a powerful developmental experience and the other factors, such as 360-degree feedback, coaching, and goal setting, that may increase the probability that learning and development will occur.

High Potentials

High potentials are those people who at various points in their careers are perceived to be potential successors to those at higher organization levels. Cope (1998) discusses the methods used for identifying and developing high potentials. Organization-specific competency models usually are the foundation for identification, and various types of assignments are used for development. The author also discusses how the companies being reported on deal with whether or not to inform the high potential about having been identified and some of the issues associated with that.

Even with a competency model, determining who is a high potential is not always easy. Ruderman and Ohlott (1990) identify possible information-processing biases in the selection of high potentials. Schaubroeck and Lam (2002) discuss biases related to similarity of personality traits among the individual, his or her manager, and his or her peers in two different cultures.

IQ is not sufficient (Gladwell, 2002), nor is strong performance in a particular function (Lombardo & Eichinger, 2000; Walker & LaRocco, 2002). Neither demonstrates conclusively that the individual can master other functions and combinations of multiple functions at higher levels of intellectual and emotional complexity. Lombardo and Eichinger (2000) suggest that learning agility, as demonstrated by performance over time in a variety of assignments, is the best way to determine if an individual is a high potential.

Annotated Bibliography

Cope, F. (1998). Current issues in selecting high potentials. *Human Resource Planning, 21*(3), 15–17.

This article summarizes the results of a workshop that addressed various methods for identifying and developing high potential candidates. Four organizations reported: Westcoast Energy, 3M, NationsBank, and a business unit from Boeing.

Each organization defined high potentials somewhat differently. Thus, a high potential in one company would not necessarily be a high potential in another. While high potential selection processes differed, each company used leadership competencies as the basis for constructive discussion and evaluation of candidates.

All four organizations provided opportunities for either special or accelerated development for their high potentials. Assignments varied, but included such things as stretch assignments, exposure to senior management, and early involvement with strategic issues.

Westcoast Energy, 3M, and NationsBank encouraged their managers to share a high potential rating with individual employees in the context of the performance review and development plan. Whether to share this information was up to the individual manager. Until recently, the Boeing business unit had kept its high potential list secret. There were several benefits from making the list public: more respect for the leadership development process, more positive employee perceptions of leadership development, and the guarantee of a rigorous process that can withstand scrutiny. Boeing had concerns about a public list related to issues such as what happens when a high potential is removed from the list and whether the employee would have a valid claim regarding an implied contract. Boeing decided to make the list public every year and to state that there was no guarantee of success or promotion. If a person was removed from the high potential list, it was the responsibility of that person's manager to inform the employee.

Some organizations have begun to create a separate list for those who don't make the high potential list, called the high professional list. These are people who are strong performers within their own specialty areas and who deserve appropriate recognition. This program was discontinued at 3M because line managers often were unsure of the distinction between high potential and high professional. NationsBank abandoned this practice as well for similar reasons. Boeing recognized this category informally.

✳ ✳ ✳

Gladwell, M. (2002, July 22). The talent myth: Are smart people overrated? *The New Yorker, 78,* 28–33.

Using Enron as the prime example, the author critiques the basic concepts proposed by consultants working for McKinsey & Company in their book, *The War for Talent.* Essentially, the McKinsey consultants found that the difference between top-performing companies and others was that the leaders of top companies were obsessed with hiring top talent, regardless of relevant experience, and then promoting and rewarding them disproportionately. While the reasons for Enron's bankruptcy are complex, the author suggests that Enron may have failed because of its talent mind-set, not in spite of it.

The author describes a culture at Enron in which talent and intelligence were rewarded for their own sake and accountability for results was minimal. Employees were ranked and placed in three groups: the A group was promoted and rewarded disproportionately, the B group was encouraged and affirmed, and the C group either was told to shape up or was shipped out. The author gives examples in which those in the A group lost millions of dollars in various ventures—apparently without needing to learn what went wrong. While Enron encouraged risk taking and tolerated mistakes, it apparently did not define expectations and measure performance effectively.

Referring to research conducted by psychologist Robert Sternberg and others, the author points out that there is little correlation between IQ and job performance. While interpersonal skills and the ability to work effectively as part of a group or team are not necessary for top performance in school, they are for top performance in most work settings.

✻ ✻ ✻

Lombardo, M. M., & Eichinger, R. W. (2000). High potentials as high learners. *Human Resource Management, 39,* 321–329.

The authors report the results of research aimed at describing key aspects of learning agility. There are four factors:

- People agility
- Results agility
- Mental agility
- Change agility

The authors say that the ability to learn from experience demonstrates that a person is a high potential. The authors use the term *learning agility* to describe this. They say further that this is demonstrated when an individual learns new skills in new situations rather than simply extending a preexisting expertise to a situation or problem. Thus a strong performer in a particular function may or may not be a high potential in the terms used by the authors.

✻ ✻ ✻

Ruderman, M. N., & Ohlott, P. J. (1990). *Traps and pitfalls in the judgment of executive potential.* Greensboro, NC: Center for Creative Leadership.

The authors examine ways individuals make judgments about the executive potential of others. They identify and discuss four information-processing strategies that may systematically distort human resource decisions and judgments of executive potential. They then suggest practices to accommodate and work with, instead of against, these distortions for the benefit of the identification process.

The authors focus on four information-processing biases:

- How evaluation questions are framed, which influences the number and type of people screened
- Categorizing people inaccurately or stereotyping
- Use of nonpredictive descriptions of job performance

• The decision maker's propensity to ignore summary data and notice concrete vivid information

The authors suggest various methods for working with these distortions to improve selection.

✳ ✳ ✳

Ruderman, M. N., & Ohlott, P. J. (1994). *The realities of management promotion: An investigation of factors influencing the promotion of managers in three major companies.* Greensboro, NC: Center for Creative Leadership.

The authors summarize the results of a study to determine how promotions are made. They found that while hard work and having ability certainly form part of the basis for promotion decisions, other factors also are critical in a significant number of cases. Those factors include being in the right place at the right time, use of promotions as signals to the organization, and use of promotions for developmental purposes.

✳ ✳ ✳

Schaubroeck, J., & Lam, S. S. K. (2002). How similarity to peers and supervisor influences organizational advancement in different cultures. *Academy of Management Journal, 45,* 1120–1136.

This article reports on a study that tested how similarity of personality traits between promotion candidates and their peers and promotion candidates and their supervisors influences promotion decisions. The study was conducted in two different cultures, one with high individualism and one with high collectivism. Work unit cultures reflected these different orientations.

In units with high individualism, personality similarity to peers was positively associated with promotion. Given the high individualism, this may seem counterintuitive. However, the authors hypothesize that in individualistic cultures there is greater potential for coordination difficulties and conflict. Therefore, smooth interaction with peers may signal a social skill that is critical for success in an individualistic culture. Those who are too individualistic (for example, those who have a distinctly different approach to problem solving) may be marginalized by the group.

In units with high collectivism, supervisor-subordinate personality similarity was a significant predictor of advancement. This was because the supervisor could trust the subordinate to do a job the way the supervisor would do it.

Demographic similarity had little influence on promotion decisions.

✳ ✳ ✳

Walker, J. W., & LaRocco, J. M. (2002). Talent pools: The best and the rest. *Human Resource Planning Journal, 25*(3), 12–14.

The authors describe some of the limitations of the principles popularized by McKinsey in "The War for Talent." Instead they propose guidelines for building and managing talent and suggest that companies utilize talent pools.

Essentially, "The War for Talent" guidelines promote the idea that having the best talent at all levels is the best way to outperform competitors. The authors say there are several problems with this approach; primary among them is that potential is difficult to measure and predict. Managers often select their best performers as top talent even though those selected may not be learning agile or have other capabilities needed to progress quickly.

The authors suggest talent pools because they allow for the development of talent for a variety of positions for individuals and give the organization more flexibility. They also remind the reader that there may be a difference between top performers and high potentials and that development of talent needs to be targeted and managed with a wide range of tools.

Succession Systems and Architecture

Books and articles in this section address key current issues associated with succession management and design and/or implementation of succession management systems and processes. Current demographic trends also are addressed.

Britt (2003) and Wells (2003) point to current demographic and other trends that indicate the number of workers aged 55 and older will increase 47 percent by 2010 and that many companies are not preparing for the wave of retirements that should begin as the baby boomer cohort begins to retire. The basic elements of a succession system for the levels below CEO are known. Rothwell (2001) provides a reference guide with many tools and resources. Eastman's 1995 bibliography lists eleven elements of an effective succession plan.

Kesler (2002) extends some of the above points and provides strategic and operational advice for designing and running a succession system, including talent reviews and identification and development of high potentials. Karaevli and Hall (2003) address similar topics, while Leibman, Bruer, and Maki (1996) take a perspective emphasizing an organizational context and, in doing so, push the discussion away from succession planning and toward succession management, a more proactive organization-wide approach.

Guenther (2004) and most other authors reinforce the importance of moving beyond replacement planning and establishing slates of candidates to a more systematic and proactive approach of utilizing succession for preparing to meet future organization needs. Charan, Drotter, and Noel (2000) provide a systematic approach for proactively building and managing the talent pipeline. Conger and Fulmer (2003) provide a similar perspective.

In "The War for Talent," Chambers et al. (1998) introduce elements of talent management: recruitment, retention, compensation, performance management, and other factors. The concepts in this article, and subsequent book of the same name, have had a broad impact in encouraging a broader view of how to manage talent. Not all authors agree with the assertions of "The War for Talent" (Gladwell, 2002, cited in the "High Potentials" section; Pfeffer, 2002). Among other things, they question the notions that individual talent trumps organizational culture and that identifying the best people is simply a matter of identifying the smartest.

The Corporate Leadership Council (2003) explicitly addresses succession within the context of an overall talent management system and shows how development, talent reviews, and other core processes can be used to support an overall succession process. Berke (2005) provides a model for organizing a succession management implementation.

Finally, the article "Exclusive Survey" (2003) points out some of the more typical barriers involved in implementing a succession system. Those barriers are cost or lack of resources (including time), internal politics, and lack of an effective performance management system.

Annotated Bibliography

American Productivity & Quality Center. (2004). *Talent management: From competencies to organizational performance*. Houston, TX: Author.
    This report presents the results of a best-practice benchmarking study focused on four broad areas of talent management:

- Senior leadership's role in talent management
- Finding talent
- Driving talent to performance
- Gauging the results of talent management

Within these areas, the report highlights the following common elements among best-practice organizations. These organizations

- Define talent management broadly
- Integrate the various elements of talent management into a comprehensive system
- Focus talent management processes on their most highly valued talent
- Have committed CEOs and senior executives who devote time to talent management work
- Build competency models to create shared understanding of the skills and behaviors the organization needs and values in employees
- Monitor talent systemwide to identify current or potential future talent gaps
- Excel at recruiting, identifying, developing, and retaining top talent, as well as performance management
- Regularly evaluate the results of the talent management process

The report provides data and company-specific examples to illustrate each point.

✳ ✳ ✳

Berke, D. (2005). Requirements for implementing a succession management system. *Mt. Eliza Business Review, 7*(2), 44–49.

The author points out that much of the literature on succession planning and management describes a best-practices model but stops short of implementation guidelines. To address this, he suggests a conceptual model for thinking through implementation. He discusses three areas that should be addressed by those who are planning to implement a succession management system:

- Roles: It is critical to clarify the people or functions that have responsibility for the various tasks associated with succession management. It is particularly important to ensure that HR does not take responsibility for setting the succession agenda and goals. This must be the job of senior management.

- Systems and processes: A succession management system has many moving parts. It is important to know what these various processes and systems are and to ensure that they are coordinated.

- Resources: Any organizational effort requires resources—time, money, and people.

✳ ✳ ✳

Britt, J. (2003). It's time to get serious about succession planning. *HR Magazine, 48*(11), 12.

The author highlights key current demographic trends as a way of demonstrating the need to pay attention to potential succession issues. Those trends include the following:

- The number of workers aged 55 and older will increase 47 percent by 2010.

- Twenty-nine percent of 428 HR professionals polled have implemented succession-planning programs.

- Ninety-four percent of 200 HR professionals surveyed say younger workers in their companies are not being prepared for advancement.

- According to a survey done by Accenture in the summer of 2003, almost half of 500 middle managers surveyed said they plan to look for a new job when the economy improves. Two-thirds of those already looking say they will increase their efforts at that point.

✳ ✳ ✳

Chambers, E. G., Foulon, M., Handfield-Jones, H., Hankin, S. M., & Michaels, E. G., III. (1998). The war for talent. *The McKinsey Quarterly, 3,* 44–57.

Citing the need and increasing difficulty of attracting and retaining superior talent, the authors studied seventy-seven companies from various industries. The companies were chosen from the top and middle quintile of their industries based on ten-year total return to shareholders. The purpose was to determine the practices differentiating high-performing organizations from average organizations in terms of recruiting, developing, and retaining talent.

The authors recommend four steps to implement an effective talent-building process.

- Make talent management a burning priority. Establish a mind-set for identifying and developing talent, hold managers at all levels accountable for fostering talent building, and strengthen HR.
- Create a winning employee value proposition. To do this, companies should tailor the jobs they have to offer to attract the type of people they need and pay what it takes to attract and retain strong performers.
- Source great talent. It is critical for a company to be clear about the kinds of people they want—and do not want—and then develop innovative methods to locate them. One method for developing criteria is to analyze current top performers. Then one can begin to recruit the desired talent using a variety of sourcing methods.
- Develop talent aggressively. To do this, the authors suggest four steps:
  - Put people in jobs before they're ready. Offer opportunities to develop talent on the job, stretching their assignments to increase capabilities.
  - Put a good feedback system in place. Let people know how they are doing and where they are headed.
  - Understand the scope of your retention problem. Inform high performers that they are appreciated, giving them a sense of belonging.
  - Move on the poor performers now. Transfer job duties or let go of poor performers.

✳ ✳ ✳

Charan, R., Drotter, S., & Noel, J. (2000). *The leadership pipeline: How to build the leadership-powered company.* San Francisco: Jossey-Bass.

The authors present an approach to developing leaders at all management levels. They point out that there are different leadership requirements at different management levels. These are related to skill, time horizons and applications, and work values. The authors describe a progression through six critical career passages from individual contributor through enterprise manager. Although these six levels apply to a large enterprise, the authors suggest that several of the levels may be combined in smaller organizations. With regard to succession, the authors suggest using the six levels as a way of assessing and developing high potentials and building and managing the pipeline to meet evolving organizational needs.

✳ ✳ ✳

Conger, J. A., & Fulmer, R. M. (2003). Developing your leadership pipeline. *Harvard Business Review, 81*(12), 76–84.

The authors summarize research conducted in collaboration with the American Productivity & Quality Center (APQC). The authors identified companies that had achieved great success in succession management. The purpose of the research was to learn how these companies differed from others in their approaches to succession management and to learn about trends in the field.

The authors identify five rules for setting up a succession management system:

- Focus on a flexible system oriented toward development and not just traditional replacement planning.

- Focus on linchpin positions—jobs that are essential to the long-term health of the organization—and manage the pipeline to ensure development opportunities and experiences.

- Have a transparent system—that is, enable employees to know how they are doing and what they need to do to reach the next step. Also enable employees to provide input on goals, experience, etc.

- Regularly measure the progress of those in the system. It is important to know whether the right people are being developed at the right pace for the right jobs. It also is important to know if there are enough people in the system to avoid stretching the pool too thin.

- Keep your system flexible and open to change. Be willing to modify it in response to feedback and to improve ease of use.

Additionally, the authors point out that succession management is not just HR's job. The CEO and executive team must demonstrate active commitment, as should the board and line management.

✳ ✳ ✳

Corporate Leadership Council. (2003). *High-impact succession management: From succession planning to strategic executive talent management.* Washington, DC: Author.

This report contains the results and recommendations of a research project for which 276 organizations worldwide provided data. The authors identify four succession risks:

- Vacancy risk—when a critical leadership position is not filled
- Readiness risk—underdeveloped successors
- Transition risk—poor assimilation of executive talent
- Portfolio risk—poor deployment of talent against business goals

Case studies provide examples of how corporations have addressed these risks. There are two case studies illustrating methods for translating business strategy into talent strategy and dealing with the possibility of key talent turnover (vacancy risk). There are three case studies dealing with accelerating development (readiness risk). There are two case studies that address effective approaches to on-boarding (transition risk). And there is one case study that addresses strategically leveraging key talent (portfolio risk).

❋ ❋ ❋

Eastman, L. J. (1995). *Succession planning: An annotated bibliography and summary of commonly reported organizational practices.* Greensboro, NC: Center for Creative Leadership.

The author provides summaries of fifty-six books and/or articles along with an essay describing eleven commonly reported practices. Those practices are as follows:

- Receives visible support from the CEO and top management
- Is owned by line management and supported by staff
- Is simple and tailored to unique organizational needs
- Is flexible and aligned with the strategic business plan
- Evolves from a thorough human resources review process
- Is based upon well-developed competencies and objective assessment of candidates
- Incorporates employee input
- Is part of a broader management development effort
- Includes plans for developmental job assignments

- Is integrated with other human resources systems
- Emphasizes accountability and follow-up

✳ ✳ ✳

Exclusive survey: HR has many ideas…but little support for succession
   preparation. (2003). *HR Focus, 80*(7), S1–S4.

   This article describes some of the obstacles HR professionals face when
implementing or supporting the implementation of a succession system as
well as recommendations for addressing the obstacles, though there are more
of the former than the latter. Major obstacles include the following:

- Cost or lack of resources
- Too many demands on time already
- Overcoming resistance or politics
- Lack of an effective performance management system

   Advice from readers centers primarily on having a clear model of
what future leaders should be and conducting accurate assessments and other
testing that is impartial. Effective training and development also are
mentioned.

✳ ✳ ✳

Guenther, R. L. (2004). Is it time to replace your replacement-planning
   strategy? *Harvard Management Update, 9*(4), 3–5.

   As the title suggests, the author highlights key succession management
practices that extend succession beyond replacement planning. Those practices include the following:

- Identify areas at the greatest risk of talent loss and develop a retention strategy.
- Develop people for a range of possible positions rather than just one
  by connecting development to likely business strategies or direction.
- For shorter-term replacements, utilize input from a variety of sources
  to determine position requirements. This will lead to a better fit
  between the candidate and organizational need; it can also discourage a manager from selecting someone who is similar to him or her.
- The CEO must focus on developing the talent within the organization and hold subordinates responsible for following through. HR
  can and should help, but ultimately it is the CEO who drives this.

✳ ✳ ✳

Karaevli, A., & Hall, D. T. (2003). Growing leaders for turbulent times: Is succession planning up to the challenge? *Organizational Dynamics, 32*(1), 62–79.

The purpose of the article is to identify and discuss elements of best practices in current succession-planning processes. To do this, the authors reviewed the policies of thirteen organizations with well-known succession-planning, talent identification, and development programs. Common elements are discussed, along with recommendations for improved succession planning.

General findings include the following: There is no one best way to identify high potentials and develop them. Those best-practices companies whose processes were formal are adopting more informal processes; the opposite also is true. Line management ownership is increasing. There is general consensus on the types of data needed to identify high potentials along with increased use of group processes and a decrease in paperwork. Development is becoming more individualized. There is an increased focus on developing talent pools rather than identifying replacements and an increased recognition of learning agility as a critical skill for leading in turbulent times.

The authors also found that executive cloning remains too prevalent and that a focus on selection of high potentials may lead to a false sense of security since it is difficult to determine what qualities might be needed for the future. They also found that the link between executive development and company strategy is weak. They conclude the article with several recommendations, including the following:

- Simplify and decentralize the process. Use information technology to support group reviews and provide data for individual feedback— which is best delivered in person.
- Design the succession management program to fit the corporate culture, which includes balancing formal and informal systems and processes.
- Stress learning and adaptability (rather than competency models) by providing on-the-job stretch assignments and learning opportunities. Pace new assignments. Provide coaching and mentoring. Build in accountability by ensuring that the individual gets feedback and that developmental plans are actually implemented.

✳ ✳ ✳

Kesler, G. C. (2002). Why the leadership bench never gets deeper: Ten insights about executive talent development. *Human Resource Planning,* *25*(1), 32–44.

This article summarizes ten insights learned through more than ten years of research and consultation with twenty-five major companies.

- The author says that traditional succession planning in the form of replacement planning is so administratively intensive that the act of completing replacement charts and other paperwork may produce a sense of accomplishment that masks the fact that nothing has happened to change the leadership readiness of the company. All that has been accomplished is the completion of paperwork. The author suggests that executives would do better by clarifying what they want their company's succession-planning process to accomplish (rather than copying systems designed for other companies like General Electric or IBM) and by creating talent pools to act as feeder groups for the leadership needs at each level.

- The author suggests that ongoing dialogue replace annual organizational reviews. Organizational reviews consist of managers at various organizational levels completing paperwork as preparation for a discussion with their managers who repeat the process for their managers. This all rolls up toward a chairman's review meeting. This approach is largely administrative and does little to advance organizational readiness. The author suggests regular review meetings as an alternative. These meetings would occur one day every quarter and the agenda would be to compare, rate, and rank high potentials against previously discussed candidates. Other elements include review of development actions. This approach encourages ongoing dialogue and may help to add value by encouraging a shared agenda and more candid discussion of candidates in the context of the company's needs.

- It is essential to establish and implement a policy that clearly deals with who owns the talent. Otherwise political dynamics between departments and the executives who lead them can hinder honest evaluation of key talent as well as the ability to make effective developmental assignments. The CEO must work with his or her executives to ensure that criteria for assessing talent are agreed upon and consistently applied and that no one be allowed to hide talent.

- The CEO must set the talent agenda. Led by the CEO, top executives must establish and implement a set of principles and philosophies that serve the overall interests of the company and directly confront political dynamics that undercut effective collaboration on the company's talent agenda. These principles can include items such as how talent will be differentiated, the role of line management in development of people, movement of people for purposes of development, etc. Many of these items will be debated and decided over time, but the CEO cannot delegate leadership in this matter.

- Assessing development potential can be very difficult. Executives must determine a candidate's fitness for positions requiring a step-function increase in the ability to manage complexity. This means executives should have a clear sense of the complexity demands of key leadership roles. The author suggests multisource ratings instead of relying on a single manager's assessment of candidate potential, which can lead to a number of problems.

- Assessing and developing talent are skills that need to be developed. Often, executives rely on their own intuition for selection, a method that may lack reliability. The author suggests that an executive team work through rating and ranking candidates. Often skilled facilitation is needed to make this work.

- Executives should not have responsibility for identifying and developing their own successors. There are two reasons: executives often select others like them and the incumbent is not necessarily the best judge of what skills and abilities will be needed in the future. In a turbulent business environment, strategy and direction may require significant change. Thus, the author suggests, executive continuity should no longer be the primary objective for succession planning. Instead, the objective should be to have ready candidates who can help move the organization in the desired direction.

- Potential leaders should be differentiated or identified early. This allows the most resources to be allocated to the best prospects. The goal is to give these candidates varied assignments over time in which levels of responsibility and complexity increase. This is most effective when followed by frequent feedback. Written performance development plans—usually part of the annual review process—can be effective only if the plans have substance and follow-up is done.

- Accountability and feedback matter. The best talent management programs utilize developmental assignments. These developmental assignments are most effective when combined with measurement and frequent feedback. Additionally, the assignments must be long enough for those assigned to see the results of their decisions, increasing accountability.

- The CEO and other line executives own the outcomes of talent development; HR owns the process. It is critical that HR support line management's ownership of the outcomes of the talent management process and avoid dominating staffing and other related decisions. Instead, HR should provide the assessment data and facilitation needed for the line to make critical talent management decisions.

※ ※ ※

Leibman, M., Bruer, R. A., & Maki, B. R. (1996). Succession management: The next generation of succession planning. *Human Resource Planning, 19*(3), 16–29.

The authors propose the adoption of succession management concepts and practices and contrast these along a number of dimensions with succession planning. Succession planning, they say, was developed in an era when the business environment was stable and much more predictable than the current highly dynamic business environment. Thus, organizations that want to stay competitive should adopt succession management practices.

The authors highlight six dimensions of succession management:

- Corporate orientation—to develop depth in leadership capability so that the organization can successfully meet unanticipated needs

- Organizational focus—determining whether an individual meets job requirements and adds value to team performance

- Outcome—focusing on regular reviews of people and organizational needs rather than a lengthy once-a-year slating process

- Assessment techniques—assessing people against a broad leadership template in which the emphasis is more on organizational vision, values, and leadership competencies than on function-related knowledge and skills. (The point here is that technical knowledge or skills are necessary but not sufficient, so 360-degree feedback is used. This reduces reliance on ratings by an individual's manager, which may reflect too narrow a perspective to be entirely useful for succession management purposes.)

- Communication—communicating openly with people about their status and development opportunities or needs and career prospects
- Selection pools—looking inside and outside the organization for appropriate successors

Four methods are suggested to help redefine the succession-planning process:

- Develop leadership templates to help close the gap between the strategic intent and current performance.
- Increase the use of talent pools and decrease the use of slating.
- Redefine the role of the senior management team to shift its focus to managing the development of the company's future leaders.
- Link development to firm-specific competencies rather than focusing on development for a specific position.

✳ ✳ ✳

Pfeffer, J. (2002, First Quarter). The talent war is a losing battle. *Strategy + Business,* pp. 11–13.

In a brief critique of the approaches popularized by *The War for Talent,* the author says that this approach is misguided because it assumes that

- Identifying the best people is easy
- Their ability will show regardless of organizational factors that may encourage or discourage excellent performance
- Organizational performance is only the sum total of individual performances
- Differentiated pay works

Using examples from sports and business, the author shows why the first three assumptions do not stand up to scrutiny. He does say that tying pay to performance can work, but that if the system is not designed correctly, differentiating pay can discourage teamwork and learning.

✳ ✳ ✳

Rothwell, W. J. (2001). *Effective succession planning: Ensuring leadership continuity and building talent from within* (2nd ed.). New York: American Management Association.

This is a reference guide providing a detailed overview of the succession planning and management (SP&M) process. The author covers the following topics:

- Factors influencing SP&M
- How to utilize competencies in the SP&M process
- How to begin and refine an SP&M program
- Development of successors
- Applying online and other technology-based approaches
- Evaluating SP&M programs

The author also provides many worksheets, charts, and descriptions of activities, all of which may be used to facilitate the SP&M process.

✳ ✳ ✳

Wells, S. (2003). Who's next? *HR Magazine, 48*(11), 45–50.

The author highlights several key elements of a succession management process and common traps.

The author makes the case for effective succession planning by

- Referring to a Society for Human Resource Management study that says that many organizations are not preparing for the impending departure of the baby boomers
- Citing a Drake Beam Morin study that shows that organizations are not preparing younger workers for senior positions
- Citing a Hewitt Associates study showing that top-performing companies measured by shareholder return are more likely to have formal development processes in place for identifying potential leaders, developing them, and tracking their performance.

With this as a context, the author cites several reasons for unsuccessful succession management efforts including lack of follow-through on implementation, lack of executive support, and overly complex, bureaucratic systems.

The author then discusses several key factors for effective succession systems: HR's role, identification of high potentials, and considerations related to communication processes for succession systems.

Those succession systems that work, she says, are integrated with a company's ongoing performance management processes. HR plays a critical role in facilitating the process by involving executive and line management in the design, analyzing and managing the data needed to monitor and support various succession processes and associated decisions, and providing expert input and advocacy.

The author highlights the acceleration pool approach used by Development Dimensions International as a means of identifying pools of people for development. With this approach, people are not part of a high potential pool. Instead they are developed to maximize their contribution to the organization.

Finally, the author discusses the pros and cons of informing individuals that they are being developed for an executive position. Companies retain maximum flexibility by not informing employees; however, lacking information about their future with the company, top performers may leave. If a company communicates this information, the author cautions that potential should be noted but no promises should be made about promotions or job guarantees.

Conclusion

The various articles and books summarized in this bibliography have addressed key elements of succession management and planning, including CEO succession, development, high potentials, and succession systems and architecture. A convenient model for organizing those elements includes the following:

- Establishing clear roles
- Determining and implementing appropriate systems and processes
- Ensuring necessary resources

Roles

Whether we are discussing succession processes at the CEO level or below that, much of the literature addresses who is supposed to do what and how they are supposed to do it. For example, many of the articles on CEO succession remind boards of directors of their role and responsibility in the succession process—as well as the appropriate roles for search firms and Wall Street analysts (Charan & Useem, 2002; Khurana, 2001). Quite simply, boards should follow well-known selection processes—understand the need and interview and select for it. Other articles encourage boards to examine assumptions about the actual roles internal or external successors play or might play and the conditions under which each might be successful (Canella & Shen, 2002; Zhang & Rajagopalan, 2004).

At lower levels, roles are equally important. Kesler (2002), as well as other writers on the subject, points out the essential differences in roles between the CEO, line management, and human resources: the CEO owns the succession agenda; the CEO and line management are responsible for the desired outcomes—often with HR support; and human resources owns the processes that support executive and line management.

Systems and Processes

Within this framework, development is only one of several core systems and processes. Others include the following:

- A competency model (Corporate Leadership Council, 2001; Lombardo & Eichinger, 2002)

- A performance management system, which builds on the competency model (Chambers et al., 1998)

- A talent review process, which builds on the competency model and data from the performance management system (Corporate Leadership Council, 2003)

- An HR information system that provides necessary reports for detecting trends and facilitating decision making (Kesler, 2002; Lombardo & Eichinger, 2002)

- An executive-level policy and review process that sets and enforces policies and goals and that identifies that outcomes are met (Corporate Leadership Council, 2003; Kesler, 2002)

When taken together, the systems and processes above act as the feeder system for identification and development of internal CEO candidates. Conger and Nadler (2004) suggest that at the most senior levels, internal candidates have at least two enterprise-wide assignments lasting three years each to finalize their development.

As noted in the introduction, CEO succession can be an orderly process in which the incumbent steps down to be replaced by an heir apparent who has been identified and groomed for the position. This is known as relay succession (Vancil, 1987). Research indicates that an internal successor tends to have a greater positive impact than an external candidate and that a successor from relay succession tends to have a greater positive impact than an internal successor who was not an heir apparent (Zhang & Rajagopalan, 2004).

Resources

Lack of sufficient resources—time, money, and people—often is mentioned as a barrier to implementation of the systems and processes named above (Corporate Leadership Council, 2003; "Exclusive Survey," 2003). Whether resources actually are the issue is another matter. Among corporations of roughly equal size and, presumably, approximately equal resources, some have implemented what might be called best-practices systems, while others have not (Berke, 2005; also see APQC, 2004, for an illustration).

It is likely that while lack of resources may be the stated reason, the real reason probably has more to do with long-held cultural beliefs about succession and development and how extensive such a process should be. Many of the authors cited in this bibliography point out how crucial it is to design a succession system that fits the culture of the organization (see Eastman, 1995, for example). Thus, while many authors describe extensive best-practices succession systems, it probably is best to remember that the best-practices system for a particular organization is likely to be the one that produces the desired outcome—whether that means building a leadership pipeline or simply focusing on the top two or three organization levels, as many organizations do.

Author Index

Title Index

Ordering Information

For more information, to order additional **CCL Press** publications, or to find out about bulk-order discounts, please contact us by phone at **336-545-2810** or visit our online bookstore at **www.ccl.org/publications**. Prepayment is required for all orders under $100.